Transitioning From A Weekend To A Warzone

Renata Morgan

Transitioning From A Weekend To A Warzone
Copyright © 2019 Renata Morgan
Voice Of Silence Publishing, Inc.

Cover Illustrator: Kelvin Gist Jr.

Cover Graphics: Kimberly Cardell

Cover Photo Provided By: Renata Morgan

ISBN: 978-0-9742545-0-0

Printed in the United States of America
10 9 8 7 6 5 4 3 2

For Online Purchases, Booking Information and other great Gift Selections, check out Renata's amazing Website: Booksabrilliant.com

Contents

Contents

Forward

Her Call To Action

She never intended to be separated from her child. She never intended to be assigned and transported to Iraq. She never intended to be shaken by bombs and rattled by live rounds. She never intended to be the witness of a suicide. She never intended to draw her weapons, as an encounter to the audacity of blatant disrespect. She never intended to absorb the pain of fellow Soldiers, as limbs were lost and lives became distorted.

She never imagined in her mind, to be anything more than a weekend warrior, on occasion and according to what she was already accustomed too.

Then all of a sudden the dynamics of her routine faced a sudden changed. A change that came without warning, without anticipation and without delay she was pulled away from her comfort zone and placed directly into her Countries War Zone.

Introduction

The Demanding Transition

"What would it feel like, being a soldier?"

I remember asking myself that question, back in 1998 and with only one way to find out, I made my decision to join the Military. After years of rejecting the recruiting officer's tireless efforts, it was as if something had clicked. Something that connected within and ignited an interest, that stirred up my curiosity. At that moment, all I could think about was how much more I would be open to listening and receive from the recruiter next phone call.

Finally, the day of anticipation had arrived and oddly enough, I can still hear the recruiter voice as he began to rattle through the scripted tactics of persuasion. Just as clear till this day, I can hear his masculine vocals rallied up for the verbal combat of rebuttals. I allowed myself to take in as much as I could digest at the time, but his wording began to target beyond my comprehensive levels, so I enforced my projected voice and expressed my willingness to enlist, in the United States Army, finally.

Continued

"I'm ready".

That simple statement changed the tone and dynamics of our conversation and eventually my life, instantaneously. Silence briefed the line, for nearly 30 seconds and the exhale of achievement, instituted a sensation of relief throughout the duration of our call.

Once my commitment was made, the next step was to review and fill out various forms of paperwork. Paperwork that at first glance, appeared to be translated through some form of foreign language. Initially, I was literally unable to make sense of the documents that were sitting before me. However, before I would sign my life away, I needed to analyze the verbiage several times over.

After I received my reassurance and elucidation to move forward, I was expected to travel to Cleveland, Ohio. Upon arrival at the Military Entrance Processing Center (MEPS), I was scheduled to take the Army Service Aptitude Battery Test, (ASVAB). This is the test, that would ultimately determine my qualifications to become a soldier in the U.S.

Continued

Military. Enthusiastically, I passed and at that point it was time to select my Military Occupational Specialty.

Having a passion for relations in the Criminal Justice field, I decided that becoming a Military Police Officer would be a perfect fit for me and reflective to my ASVAB scores, my MOS was official. Praises going up, as I was one step closer to begin my Military career as an MP.

The next phase was to ensure, that I was physically fit enough to endure the rigorous routine expectancies which the Military required. To confirm that this was the case, I had to take a physical that was administered by a Military Dr. and without a doubt in mind, I managed to complete and pass it with flying colors. Conquering the check off list of acceptance one by one, I was now about to face a moment that would alter my life, forever.

Continued

I remember going into a room that was staged with many Military personnel seated before me. As I looked ahead, not quite sure of what to expect, a deep piercing voice of insensitive authority spoke out from the most odious facial expression amidst them all:

"Raise your right hand and repeat after me", he commanded.

It was at that moment that I began to question, if I was making the right decision. It was at that moment, that my thoughts began to rattle and battle, back and forth through my mind. It was at that moment, that my life would come to a complete stand still for at least 60 seconds. It was at that moment that I drifted off into a numbness, unable to verbalize a sound, as I surveyed the opportunities that were just a few outspoken words away. It was at that moment, that I deeply reflected on the commitment that I would agree to and if it would be adequately worthwhile.

Continued

See, I'm a woman of research and even prior to the recruiter calling me back, I took the initiative to converse with several individuals that had been and were still actively serving in the Military. Out of everyone that I had spoken with about their experience, some simply replied that it wasn't too bad. Still and all, the majority seemed to have sized me up and took it upon themselves to count me out immediately. Commenting narratively, that they were not sure if I would make it and suggesting that I should reconsider, as they assumed it might not be what's best for me.

High above my chest, my right hand remained raised in the air and as I replayed those statements within my thoughts, my mental paradigm began to shift. It was at that moment the numbness began to fade and I instantaneously became intrigued, by the gratification of a challenge conquered. Before I knew it, the repetition of words rolled out of my mouth with ease and I had now become a soldier, in the United States Army.

Continued

Sworn in and ready to serve, my tasks over the next few weeks would have me assigned to a Military Police Company where I was expected to report and complete training, one weekend a month and two weeks out of a year. The monthly trainings exposed me to detailing several subjects, leading but not limited to the following: How to conduct a proper Preventative Maintenance Checks & Services (PMCS), on a Military vehicle, transmitting and receiving information over a Military radio, properly clearing a building, search and seizures of a vehicle, how to detain an individual, the proper steps and level of force used when detaining individuals and weapons qualifications linked with other ongoing alternative trainings.

Another vital portion of the Company training involved our health, as we were required to maintain a level of fitness, to remain in the Military. These trainings were executed through the form of a physical fitness test administered periodically, as well as within the two weeks course, of our annual training sessions. Ideally, for me this was a

Continued

piece of cake, and all thing's surrounding my life were just simply beautiful. I was able to conduct myself as a normal citizen outside of the Military, while at the same time obtain the experience of being a true soldier.

Everything was smooth and steady in motion, as I advanced into the third month of drills with my Company. Then all of a sudden, the handle that I had on life shifted, as I was approached by my Platoon Sergeant, whom informed me that I would be soon leaving out for Basic Training. In full details, my Platoon Sergeant explained to me that in a matter of weeks, I would be taking off and reporting to Fort McClellan, Alabama which is where I was expected to complete four long months of strenuous Military training.

Fort McClellan, Alabama

Chapter 1

Separation from my Company took place in the middle of spring, as I would be detached from my routine lifestyle and assembled amongst a new assortment of soldiers, for Basic Training. Doing my best to be prepared, I had communicated with other soldiers from within my Company, who had just completed Basic Training a few weeks prior. My intentions were to receive insight and foresight on what I was to expect. Over all, the embellishments from the experiences shared with me, appeared to be nothing like the venture that I was about to face, personally.

From A Weekend, To A Warzone
Renata Morgan

I remember being bussed through the premises for nearly an hour, surrounded by the thickening of a wooded area displaying nothing but trees. Trailing this blueprint into the Barracks, my anxieties were triggered as I began to wonder if we would be pulling over at any moment to pitch tents. Of course, I could not confirm the thoughts of anyone else, but I was not ready to live in tent city for the next several months.

Finally, the bus stopped and when the doors opened a male Drill Sergeant stepped forward to address us. His voice greeted us with a calming coolness and with relief, I exhaled my thoughts of intensity, presuming that the experience would not be as bad as previously anticipated. Although to my un-expectancy, once I stepped off the bus with a green duffle bag attached to the front and one to the back of me, I quickly realized that we were a load of fresh meat for a shark attack.

I'm not sure where the welcoming Drill Sergeant disappeared to, but as we stood on the camp grounds, ferociously swarmed by a squad of treacherous Drill Sergeants derived directly from the pits of hell, it was as though

From A Weekend, To A Warzone
Renata Morgan

every bone in my body had become frozen in terror. Five different Drill Sergeants, yelling out five different directives at the same time and expecting each command to be attentively followed, upon immediate request. This is not what I signed up for, as I then looked down to my feet, clicked my heels together three times and voiced repeatedly, "There is no place like home".

Unfortunately, my reality was that my feet were not embraced by ruby slippers. Yet, quite the contrary they were laced in Army Boots and rather I wanted it to be or not, this was exactly what I had signed up for.

Basic Training consisted of five phases, which I had the opportunity to learn multiple skill sets, throughout various forms of instructive teachings and tactical techniques. Our educational focal points stemmed from classroom settings, to outdoor ranges, MP Combat support sites, weaponry training, leadership skills, gas chambers, map reading and many other defensive tactics.

From A Weekend, To A Warzone
Renata Morgan

Rigorously, as the days went on and time rolled by, many things began to come with ease and even the Drill Sergeants began to come around with a lot less aggression. Although from the start, it was like being trained by a relentless team of men and women, that presented themselves as some of the meanest, roughest, toughest, loudest and most intolerable people that I had ever been in contact with throughout my life.

Precise and direct, every soldier in my Company was required to respond swiftly to the Drill Sergeants commands, without hesitation. We were supervised to handle situations with no excuses, and explanations were absolutely unacceptable. In fact, each Drill Sergeant expected results at demand or instructed us to drop into a push up position, until they felt uncompromisingly satisfied.

Clearly at my entry of Basic Training, I was unaware to so much of what was taking place or why, for that matter. But with much respect, by the end the cycle, I was able to develop a concise overview. The intentions

From A Weekend, To A Warzone
Renata Morgan

were not to break us down, but to build our instinctive nature for preparation, discipline, attention to detail and most importantly, self-determination.

For me, the gaining of so much knowledge and bonding with so many great people over that four months period, was amazing. In spite of all the greatness captured, the one thing that embedded itself with me the most, was the Drill Sergeants voice yelling out: "You better make sure you're paying attention because one day, you'll be going to WAR!!!"

Not likely, one would think as a Military Police Officer in the Army National Guard, but that's exactly what happened to me in the year of 2003. My monthly once a weekend and yearly two weeks of training would be no more, as the proposed orders to become an Active Duty Soldier, for the next 365 days would be surprisingly awaiting me.

The Call

Chapter 2

"Yeah, right."
That's exactly how I replied to the caller, as I sat comfortably on my couch watching television.

"You must be kidding me."
I uttered as I hung up the phone, on what I gathered to be a prank.

"What a character."
I mumbled faintly, as I continued to relax within the serenity of my private domain.

Squad Leader my tail, I thought as I sighed out a humph of annoyance. Clearly, someone had too much time on their hands. Calling me

From A Weekend, To A Warzone
Renata Morgan

during the wee hours of the evening, talking about report to my Company within 24 hours. Absurdly speaking of an Operation Order, that instructed me to be deployed for a mission in Iraq.

"Yeah, right." Again, I proceeded in thought to myself, only to receive a call with the same orders several hours later. At that point, I began to verbally express my irritation to the shenanigans and commented that I would not be answering any future calls. Sure enough, my phone rang and as previously proclaimed, I did not answer.

About 45 minutes went by and I received another phone call. That time I answered, heated up and ready to spew out a few choice words. Furthermore, before I had a chance to speak, all I could hear was: "Specialist Morgan, this is not a drill. This is a real live situation and you need to report to the Company, immediately."

The Order was real. The information was delivered as a directive from the higher commands. And the specifics were generated

Renata Morgan

by a leader, whom detailed this operation particularly, as Operation Iraqi Freedom.

That's when my heart fell to my feet. Suddenly, I began to encounter an out of body experience, akin to the likeness of being chased down by my shadow from Basic Training. It was as if, I had been invaded by the memory of marching in formation with a rucksack full of boulders adhered to my shoulders and weighing heavily upon my back.

Mentally, my thoughts started racing into a million different directions. Physically, I could not make a move or speak a sound. I felt completely lifeless for what seemed to be hours in passing and eventually, after hearing a repeated hello, I responded: "I'm here, and I'll be there shortly."

Conflicting to what I had spoken out of my mouth, there was no way that I was going overseas. I had a Son, who was still a toddler at the time and the idea of separating from him, was just preposterous. I couldn't even begin to imagine what he would think with his Mommy being there one day and gone the next. On top of that, I would have to figure out

From A Weekend, To A Warzone
Renata Morgan

how to explain to my family, that I would be leaving the United States, to go fight in a War in Iraq.

Wrestling in my thoughts to make sense of it all, I finally built up enough strength to proceed to my Company. When I arrived, I was moving in snail motion, slowly easing out of my vehicle with no urgency to enter the non-stop commotion, that was awaiting me on the inside.

It was like walking into a mad house of systematic dysfunction, as orders were being given right and left. Equipment was spread out over the entire drill floor, soldiers were pacing back and forth and there I was positioned as if a statue, smack dab in the middle of it all. Overwhelmed by the chaos, the surrealness around me was cinematic to state the least.

"Was this really happening?"

"Were we really in preparation, to go fight in someone else's country?"

From A Weekend, To A Warzone
Renata Morgan

I'm not sure what exactly made me snap out of it, but after a tumultuous ten minutes, reality finally set in and I knew that this was not a drill.

For the next few hours, the Company would operate as an over exerted assembly line. Short circuiting through an assortment of multiple parts, that no one could quite get a handle on. Mounds of paperwork were being distributed rapidly, families were baffled in confusion and soldiers were shamelessly disoriented. It was a sound asylum turned upside down, by the constant commotion that circulated throughout the room.

"Why us?"

"Why were we the ones to receive the call?"

"We didn't volunteer for this mission?"

"Who's responsible for this decision?"

Questions were asked, but none of them mattered because despite the process, we were the ones specifically selected and chosen to fulfill the command. What did matter was that

Renata Morgan

we had 72 hours to get our affairs in order and spend some quality time with our families because once that time was up, we would be departed for 365 days.

After leaving the Company that evening, I contemplated not going back. I just couldn't wrap my mind around detaching from my only child, whom at the time hadn't even reached his terrible two's yet. Being away would cause me to miss out on so much of his critical growing moments and that was not a sacrifice, that I was ready to make.

Only completing 6 years in the Military, the idea of retiring hadn't crossed my mind, so going AWOL did not matter. What mattered, was my little prince that I held tightly in my arms while singing sweet lullabies, until his precious pint size body was at peace. While rocking him back and forth, I also began to mentally materialize the outcome that I would have to face, from the consequences of going AWOL and honestly, it wasn't worth the ordeal.

From A Weekend, To A Warzone
Renata Morgan

As a MP, I reflected on the times when I had to knock on another soldiers' door and the extremities which they were subjected to, was not a game. I had to consider my options and decide if I was ready to spend time behind bars, for intentionally refusing to show up to a mandatory deployment, or was I going to give my Son and family many heroic stories upon my return. I quickly placed my faith in option two and began implementing the necessary steps for getting my affairs in order, before taking off for my assignment.

Approaching the 72 hours mark, it was time for my Company to be bused to the Airport in Toledo, Ohio. Our families were there to see us off and I swear I must have shed a bucket of tears, as I said my good-byes.

When the time came for me to release my Son to his Father, my tears were an uncontained overflow. With one foot on the plane and one foot off, holding my Son next to my heart, my grip was inseparable as it took everything in my body and soul, to unravel him from my arms.

From A Weekend, To A Warzone
Renata Morgan

It wasn't long before we took off to fly through the friendly skies and I was in a daze. Unable to think, my body was there, but my mind had become withdrawn and I had no desire for interaction. Shortly into the flight, my eyes began to close as I voyaged off into somnolence with dreams centered around returning into the arms of my Son, instantly.

After several hours of floating through the blue skies and white clouds, I was awakened by the turbulence of the plane, descending for landing. Arriving safely, we had finally made it to Fort Bragg, North Carolina where we would commence our preparation, to execute the beginning of our mission for Operation Iraqi Freedom.

Fort Bragg, North Carolina

Chapter 3

The sound of the blades from the aircraft slowly came to an end, as I continuously tried to make sense of why we were the soldiers, chosen to be called for such an assignment. After all, we were only fit for training once a month. We were the weekend warrior's, not the active duty soldiers, designed for such missions. At least that's how I analyzed it, but clearly, I was wrong.

Still shocked and in disbelief with looks of baffled infuriation, each soldier exited the aircraft one by one. Once off the plane, we scrambled into formation for accountability and then we headed to a bus that was purposed to escort us to a mobilization area, designated for incoming Company's. Already familiar with the hurry up and wait process from previous experiences, I knew that the day would be composed of extended hours.

One of the first briefing's given to us, simplified that we should not become comfortable, due to the facts that we would only monopolize the base for 96 hours. The briefing went on to relay, that at that time we would then evacuate into the next phase of our mission. Those instructions were great news to my ears, rationalizing that the sooner we would leave, the sooner we could return and once again reunite with our love ones.

For the next few days, I would sit through countless briefings and the ordinance of do's and don'ts, pertaining to the Fort Bragg Installation. Trainings would also be implemented, so the days appeared to be effortlessly ending.

Time continued ticking away, with the infamous 96th hour turning into the 97th and we were still on the grounds of Fort Bragg. The sunrise began to elapse into the sunset, as

Renata Morgan

soldiers were then amassed into formation, to be enlightened about our extension on the instillation.

Right then an eruption of frustration took over me. I was ready to leave, so that we could complete the mission and get back home. Nonetheless, the news given meant that we would have a delay in our return.

Now the days had turned into weeks, the weeks turned into months and I began to entertain the thoughts that maybe our orders had been revoked. I concluded in my mind, that maybe we weren't the chosen ones. Exploring those possibilities in my thoughts stimulated me because that meant that I could arrange to visit with my Son, and that's exactly what took place.

Commencing to generate phone calls home, I began to set up arrangements for my Son to fly down to North Carolina, to see me. My adrenaline was bursting at the mere fact that I would be able to look into the beautiful eyes of my Son, once more and recapture the missed moments thus far. Finally, the anticipated weekend arrived. Intensely fueled by

From A Weekend, To A Warzone
Renata Morgan

excitement shifting through my body the entire drive, I jetted down the interstate envisioning my first reaction, over and over again.

When I pulled up to the doors of the airport, there came walking out, this little guy with a smile that would have my heart racing at an accelerated rate. Within seconds my eyes were filled with tears, causing my cheeks to become massively drenched. Jumping out of the vehicle, faster than a bolt of lightning at blazing speed, I grabbed him so tight that I could see he was gasping for air through the swelling of veins, in his tiny pupils. It was a moment of total bliss for me, as his limbs seemed to have cloaked around my whole body and I felt the embracement of my baby boy, yet again.

Once I got back on the interstate after making my way through the congested airport traffic, it was a challenge to remain focused on the road, as my eyes continued to drift away in pure admiration. I was absolutely humbled to witness the wonderfully made masterpiece of a human being, seated next to me.

From A Weekend, To A Warzone
Renata Morgan

Within a few months of separation, my Son had graduated from saying a few words at a time, to now articulating full sentences. He made demands that I was incredibly unaware that he knew anything about, but they were followed. One thing for sure was that, my little tyke had become a fan of basketballs, so at the dismount of every store, if the object was round and bouncy and caught his attention, he left out with it in hand.

Over the course of the weekend, we traveled through several cities in North Carolina, enjoying every moment spent. We enjoyed parks, movies, arcades, bowling, go-cart riding, and adventures at the boardwalks all within the time span of 4 days.

I didn't receive much sleep at all that weekend, but when we did wind down and he shut his little eyes, mine were very much wide open. I watched over my Son, as he was peacefully resting, and I treasured every breath he would inhale and release. Cherishing each second, like the last particles of sand shifting through an hour glass, the time had come for my Son to travel back to Ohio and neither of us was enthused.

From A Weekend, To A Warzone
Renata Morgan

Before driving back to the airport, I explained to my Son in the most simplified terms, about the reality in which we were about to endure. I needed him to know what I was doing, where I was going and when I expected to return. I then placed his hand over my heart and placed my hand over his.

"Yes mommy."
My Son replied, after I asked him if he could feel the thump in my chest.

It was a soulful moment, as I looked directly into the eyes of my Son with passion and fortitude. I was determined to help him comprehend the best that I could, as he stared at me with confusion in his eyes.

"My world is a better place because of you."
I went on to tell him and to further inform him that:

"No matter the time nor length of separation, we will always share the same heartbeat."

From A Weekend, To A Warzone
Renata Morgan

I spoke from a need to reinforce in my Son that:
"No matter where you go or what you do, Mommy is always with you."

After our conversation, we embraced for what seemed to be a lifetime, then we packed up and in the warm breeze, we drove. Before I could get back to the training area, I received a phone call from my Squad Leader, stating that we had a meeting and I needed to report to the Platoon area within the hour.

Once I made it to the base, I gathered amongst other soldiers that began to surround the area, expecting to hear what our training exercise would consist of for the following day. In the meantime, everyone was laughing and sharing stories about the amazing moments that were experienced over the weekend.

Finally, the 1st Sergeant walked up and demanded everyone's attention. When he started speaking, the information that he revealed was great. On the other hand, as he went on, it was like a missile had landed in the room with the news that we all dreaded to hear.

From A Weekend, To A Warzone
Renata Morgan

"Pack all your belongings because in the next 48 hours, we will be departing from Fort Bragg and heading to Iraq."

When I heard those words, my thoughts spent out in ways that could not be contained and in an uncontrollable motion, I fainted. My body became weak and my feet were swept from under me, but mercifully, the swift abilities of a fellow soldier prevented my total collapse to the ground.

At that point, there was no second guessing that this was the real deal and any thoughts of my Company possibly not being the chosen ones, had left my mind. Ready or not, the countdown was in full effect while our final hours approached.

After our meeting was adjourned, it was time for us to disassemble and fulfill the obligations requested, prior to the 17 hour flight. This was it, I thought to myself as I fell to my knees in prayer and kissed the United States soil before boarding the aircraft.

Heavenly Father,
Bless us to return back to the
United States, the same way we are
leaving, in one piece
Amen

Touch Down Overseas

Chapter 4

The aircraft whispered through the skies, gliding throughout what seemed to be mounds of Charmin puffed clouds and the daunting fiery rose sunset that once appeared was no more, as the mechanics of our aerial charter began to descend. Ferociously, the view transitioned into a catastrophic scene of vicious winds and dust storms, provoked by the squealing wheels that landed us amidst the blistering grounds of the Middle East.

Scouting the area from where I was positioned, my eyes noticed nothing other than complete isolation. Engaged and not yet knowing exactly what to expect nor what to

Renata Morgan

think at that moment, my mind couldn't evolve to see anything more, than 364 additional days of recycled seclusion.

While I was departing the aircraft, I repetitiously rehearsed the interjected message from which the Drill Sergeant verbalized:

"You better make sure you're paying attention because one day, you'll be going to war."

And there I stood, confronted by the candor of that vigorously dispatched statement.

Still not fully certain of what was taking place, I began to wonder if we had just abruptly invaded the unidentified territory of our enemies. Yet, it was just a thought in mind, as I moved forward with no questions asked. Attentively on guard and ready for command, the echelon was in formation to maneuver one soldier in front of another with weapons secured in one hand, adjoined by boxes of live round ammunition in the other.

Seeking the whereabouts of a confined area, I quickly advanced on the backside of a sand mound, in the potential event that direct fire

From A Weekend, To A Warzone
Renata Morgan

would manifest. As I sat loading several magazines of live ammunition and stuffing them in the ammo pouches of my protective vest, my mind went back to the great Country of America.

My thoughts went into recollection of me being in the room, where I raised my right hand and I ideally reversed all steps, that led up to this moment. Of course, my reality was that there was no time for deliberation because indeed, I had taken the oath and now it was time to execute the mission.

The wee hours of day break began closing in and we were compiled into a holding area where only a few hours of sleep would be captured, before it was time to pack up and reassemble. Advancing through the desert would be like an endless voyage, so I filled my stomach with the crisp salivating taste of a Meal Ready to Eat, (MRE), before striking out for the unknown.

We drove for miles before witnessing what was perceived to be a flock of camels appearing ahead of us in an array of haze. It would be hours more into the journey, where the appearance of other forms of transportation would be noticed. Essentially, it felt like a scene from a movie. At any rate, the difference was that the authenticity of this script, was from an unscripted reality in which I was one of the main characters.

Fleeting through the pavement of the Middle East, our convoy of Military vehicles trailed past massively built abandoned homes, and deserted buildings that had been left unoccupied. The scene was like a Western, with a dead zone of store fronts, that appeared to be at some point excelling in revenue.

Sluggish in our movement, we gradually placed one vehicle bumper in front of the other, until we came to an abrupt stop. At this point, we had reached the entrance of a gate that was guarded by a division of Iraqi Troops, towering our vehicles with AK47's and machine guns, along with insignia written in a script that would be incomprehensible to our American eyes.

After being halted at the gate for what seemed to be a decennium, a gentleman wearing a long tunic and open toed sandals

Renata Morgan

would approach the convoy and one by one motion us through the gate, at which time I considered to be the transformation into the dark side.

The Birth Of Camp Anaconda

Chapter 5

Accompanied down the asphalt of a life-sized sand box, we were directed to the location of a building that resembled a dome, but seemingly structured to hold an aircraft. Mumbling amongst ourselves, we expected to see a Military Aircraft that would fill the space of this gigantic open area, but ironically this Company of men and women would make this our home for the next several months.

Once inside, we initially considered that there was no way an entire Company of soldiers could be accommodated within the walls of this cement sculpture. Despite the circumstances, with bare luxuries we found a way to construct the open field of nothingness, that stretched out for several hundred feet, into our own.

Without delay, we began with unloading the sensitive items which included: weapons, ammo, sincgars, protective masks, night vision goggles and all other equipment that was inscribed with a serial number. The Company would then be divided into four sections, with Headquarters covering one corner and the Platoons occupying the other three.

My Platoon was the first to be assigned, for all Quick Reaction Force Missions, (QRF). Declaring that in fifteen-minute intervals, we would be responsible for rapidly reacting to developing situations and collaborating with other Military Units, in need of further assistance.

After glancing over my personal designated area, that stretched about the size of 2 M16's in length and the same distance in width, I began arranging my personal belongings which wasn't much at all. Then came the assembling of the ever so comfortable, thin green layer of lavishness, that happened to be handcrafted

From A Weekend, To A Warzone
Renata Morgan

from the finest selection of canvas material attached with six sturdy metal brackets. No, it wasn't the posturepedic mattress I envisioned absorbing, but needless to say, that I was so thrilled to absorb my body into that plush contraption night after night, after night.

Clearly the amenities or lack thereof, were not what I was use too. Although realistically, this was just one of many life changing extremities, that I would be forced to endure.

After being diligently engaged for the greater fragment of the day, exhaustion had landed its way into my tireless body. As I laid across my cot, my pupils began to fill with moisture from the uncertainty of not knowing if I could survive being in this deserted jungle. Nevertheless, the thought of me returning home once again, gave me the strength to alleviate such contemplation as my mind drifted off into rest.

"Get up, we have to go. We have a mission and you have fifteen minutes to be outside with your gear, ammo and weapon systems."
    It was 1:30 a.m. and those were the whispering words that I had been awakened

From A Weekend, To A Warzone
Renata Morgan

by, as my Squad Leader continued to shake me into consciousness. I can recall rubbing my eyes with my mind still in a trance and all I could think was: "Where could we possibly be going at this time of the morning?"

Apprehensive about getting my belongings together, I was afraid of what would happen next because I had no idea of what would be announced, once I was standing under the darkened moonlight.

As the operation order was being read, I was terrified, here I am a driver in an unknown terrain and we were about to be on the search for the enemy. My knees almost buckled, but I held my composure because I couldn't allow my fellow soldiers to witness the distress of my heart pulsating uncontrollably. And although no one would speak out to say anything, I'm sure they experienced corresponding feelings quivering through the limbs, which kept their bodies tranquil.

Twelve soldiers' in three Humvee's, with an arsenal that could take over a city in its entirety, exchanged radio communications and headed to the front gate, where we nervously

From A Weekend, To A Warzone
Renata Morgan

awaited to be given our next directive. Prayers one after the other flooded my mind, as we appeared to be sitting ducks waiting for the all clear, to exit Camp Anaconda.

I was the driver, so my eyes would be expanded to their extremity with the night vision goggles mounted on my Kevlar, as I examined the outside surroundings for any suspicious or unusual activity. Meanwhile, the gunner in the turret would scan the rear and my team leader would monitor radio traffic.

Before we knew it an hour had passed, then two and eventually the third with our locality not budging an inch. As the fourth hour approached, the Squad Leader narrated for the vehicles to navigate back to our living area and stage the vehicles, for the next mission.

The retraction was stated to be a result of adversary compliance, but all I could think about was: "What rocket scientist surmised a plan, for 12 soldiers' to be awakened at the wee hours of the dawning, embellished in full battle rattle and flee to the front gate, to stare at the moonlight for numerous hours."

From A Weekend, To A Warzone
Renata Morgan

Honestly, I couldn't wait to shake the hand of the genius that mandated our return. Because while we were assembled at the gate, my intuition meditated on the fact that, if I had advanced beyond the gates outside perimeter, that day would be my final glance at Camp Anaconda.

Shaken by the thought of the alternative, once back in my personal area, I fell to my knees and bowed my head to deliver a repeated Thank You. Surely, there would be many unpredictable days ahead, but I was afraid that that day would have ultimately been an unquestionable reservation, for my annihilation.

Inside The Foreign Walls
Of Affliction

Chapter 6

Being one of the first Company's to access
the camp, we started from ground zero,
Nothing. While one Platoon resumed at the
ready for QRF missions at all times, the other
spent their days keeping the inside perimeter
safe and the third Platoon worked diligently, to
enhance the outside hygiene areas of the
Company. They would begin by building
suitable showers, then bearable restrooms.

Imagine, installed outside of your home, a 6
x 4 diameter sized wooden box with the top of
the box comprised with a complete opening
and a water hose circulating from the top.
Then picture, the water hose being placed
inside of a water jug with fifteen small holes,

punctured in the bottom of the jug to symbolize a sprinkler system with a string attached. Now, visualize yourself relying on the two minutes of lather and rinse, that's controlled for the sake of conserving the water usage for others.

Proportionately, two more wooden boxes would be submerged side by side, with a steel drum gas barrel condensed by the middle to make two equals, place a toilet seat over the top and this is what would be used to release yourself.

Subsequently, after the barrel had been occupied by human waste within a 24-hour period, the soldier on duty would then remove the barrel to burn and stir the waste in 45-minute intervals, in order for it to be consumable for usage once again.

Could you imagine, the aroma of 150 plus body fluids emerged in a barrel that must be inhaled, until its existence has been made to disappear?

I would expect that you couldn't, and neither could I because you can't imagine

From A Weekend, To A Warzone
Renata Morgan

something that's actually taking place in real time. It would be several months before contractors would start transposing various hygiene stations throughout the camp, but until then we would be stuck gratifying our own.

To top it off, we were without satellite service connections, therefore sending and receiving mail would consist of a forty-five day turn around. Talk about survival of the fittest, I would state that we ranked number one indisputably.

Usually, the days would come and go with a swift consistency, as they seemed to have materialized in dissolution. However, on this particular day, thing's would go a bit different. It was just past the peak of the morning and I was completing my business in the restroom when the sound of a loud BOOM, vibrated the inside of my eardrum with deafening force. Thank goodness, I was already hovering over the latrine or my uniform would've been soaked in a mixture of urine and human waste.

Before gathering my pants over my knees, a second BOOM would be heard raging from the

From A Weekend, To A Warzone
Renata Morgan

elevation of the unforeseen. Through all the distress of screaming and yelling, I managed to make it from the latrine executing the 3 to 5 second rush technique, as everyone grabbed their Kevlar's and proceeded to submerge under concealment.

We were being attacked by the enemy in broad daylight. Mortars were being launched in our direction without interruption. This indirect fire device, used to propel explosive shells, could be launched from close proximity, or as far out as 14,000 meters and the active shooters were scattered in between.

The soldiers in our Company were fortunate enough not to withstand any direct hits, but the shrapnel from the explosive did make its way to the back side of our living area. The Company alongside of our vicinity wouldn't be so lucky, as a few soldiers suffered some lost limbs and were rushed to the medic station, to later be announced as (Survivors Of The Wounded).

The enemy had been spotted by a Black Hawk that soared the upper atmosphere, but not for long as the sniper would zoom in and

Renata Morgan

embody the assassins' physique dead on. As uncomfortable as it was, I slept with my Kevlar on that night and contemplated leaving Camp Anaconda, to go on an ocean voyage until I reached the USA. Of course, I didn't have a well thought out plan, but I figured that I wouldn't mind suffering a few bites here and there, from various water creatures.

What I did think about, was making it home alive and being in that camp one more day, I wasn't sure if that was a possibility. Although in my rationality, I knew that it would take more than my weapon systems and a map that I couldn't comprehend, to overcome my journey of escape. I wasn't pleased about it, but I knew that I had no choice, other than to withstand the misfortune, as the countdown of the days continued.

The missions of escorting the high-profile supremacy, from one location to the next had resumed and it was much disheartening. We would ride through villages where homes had been relinquished and we witnessed children petitioning for any or all, of the soldier's belongings for miles. We rode past huge

From A Weekend, To A Warzone
Renata Morgan

impurity holes in the ground, resembling the size of a small pool, but were used for bathing instead.

We also found ourselves becoming accustomed to securing the scenes of accidents, including those of soldiers who had committed suicide. Obviously, the anticipation of traumatic catastrophes, was not something that you would be waiting to take place, but that reality was a frequent and sad truth.

When you're looking in the face of a soldier, as they are excited about sharing their life stories and you hear the animation of excitement roaring up in their tone, you begin to feel like somehow you have embedded yourself in their storyline. You surround their attention with your presence, for the length of time needed to express any outlets of stress, all the while you're engaging in the routine of cleaning weapons.

Now, proceed to envision wrapping up the weapon cleaning process and the conversation comes to an end, with the anticipation of seeing one another the next day. Well, that's exactly what didn't happen.

From A Weekend, To A Warzone
Renata Morgan

Astounded by the misfortune of grief, as I began to initiate movement towards my vehicle, I turned around to say good-bye and my eyes were in remorse as to what was witnessed. The muzzle of an M16 had been pointed to the side of the upper abdomen and the trigger had been pulled, causing the young soldier to be laid out lifeless.

Instinctively, as I thought that I had a mound of problems and was on the verge of a nervous breakdown, my life was superb compared to the one that had just been taken. It was at that moment, I realized that the outside of the human body can glitter like gold, but the inside could be pervaded with the turmoil of many dark secrets.

The cover up definitely had me convinced that there were no concerns, but in all actuality, there was so much going on that it was invisible to the naked eye. Sometimes it's difficult to decipher an individual at face value which is why it's important to understand what's going on in the inside of the book, oppose to just glancing at the cover.

From A Weekend, To A Warzone
Renata Morgan

Despite the trauma fused calamities, my assignments continued as our travels through the treacherous city of Bagdad, to fulfill overnight missions converted from seldom to habitual. Along the way, every stop composed of five minutes or greater, required soldiers in the convoy to egress the vehicle and pull a 360-degree perimeter, for the protection of the territory.

One particular morning while in route, chaperoning a physician to the medical center, our convoy encountered a disturbance as we came to a bridge crossing. Aware of their fearless nature, we understood that as a ritual, the Iranians did not value life as much and were not afraid to cease their existence, for a sacrificial execution to withdraw the lives of others', upon demand.

The incident involved a child that stood begging for food, while the parents were standing at a distance and concentrated on the number of vehicles, as well as personnel within our convoy.

Once the child began to proceed towards the vehicles, our weapons were drawn and we

From A Weekend, To A Warzone
Renata Morgan

continued to gesture for the child to get back.
Without hesitation, an automatic transition of
tension was amplified as we were now facing
the sorrowful pleas of a mother and child,
soliciting desperately for nourishment. Enticed
by their insistent request, the Command of the
convoy commenced to relinquish a box of
MRE's.

It was at that instance, the father took a few
steps forward. He slowly pulled up his tunic
and surely enough, strapped to his body were
enough explosives to demolish our entire
entourage. No, we did not shoot to kill, but we
did shoot to wound.

Our lives were saved that day, as another
insurgent would take it upon himself to
breathe his last breath. And although I must
state, that at no time was it painless to witness
someone take their own life, it was always
rewarding to infiltrate movement with the
identical number of soldiers, retracing back
into the gates of the Great Anaconda.

That evening, the nightmare of a vigorous
attack on my Company, had awakened my
body out of its slumber. Assuredly, I am by far

From A Weekend, To A Warzone
Renata Morgan

adherent when it comes to hallucination, but to glance across my living area and distinguish that heart rates of my fellow soldiers were still pumping throughout the room, provided me with great reassurance.

As the sun made its way over the chromatic horizon, I adjusted my eyes towards the luminous beam of light and sprawled out of my luxurious, resemblance of a bed. In that same moment, I encountered memory lane once again, with thoughts of being back home in the presence of my love ones.

It seems as if, when you have been silenced from the breeze of fresh air, the chirping of flocking birds, rain drops hitting the window seal and the trees sprouting into elevation, surrounded by the blossoming of colorful flowers, you then learn to appreciate the beautiful aspect of nature.

Intrigued by the reflective delightfulness, I began to think of how such circumstances constituted the lack of delicacy, when you are forced to be detached from them. However, for a split second my paradise consisted of a capsulation which included all of those things, aforementioned. Abruptly, the silence was broken by the capturing sound of several Army Tanks and tankers, with soldiers waving good-bye as they were making their way to clear customs, before their return to the USA.

After receiving another Operation Order, it wouldn't be long before my Company would exchange a majestic salute to Camp Anaconda, but our destination wouldn't be the States. Unfortunately, we weren't that lucky, instead our directives indicated that the procedure for our next destination would be the chaotic Camp Caldwell.

Chaotic Camp Caldwell

Chapter 7

Soldiers worked swiftly to initiate the load plan and ensure that we would encounter Camp Caldwell before night fall. The diligent efforts granted movement to be made just after noon day and as we embarked onto the next assignment, we cleared our living area of anything not secured to the walls and placed them in the vehicles for departure.

Traveling the bi-ways through Baghdad's several cities, towns and villages, we only stopped for the purpose of emergencies. Eventually, we began to gain sight on a huge multi-colored desert sign that was positioned to greet us with a warm welcome, 200 feet ahead.

From A Weekend, To A Warzone
Renata Morgan

As we proceeded to inch our way towards the gates of Camp Caldwell, my nostrils were awakened with an aroma that my taste buds had been lacking for what seemed to be decades. I took a deep breath and released a mouthwatering exhale, from the idea of savory seasoned poultry, baked to perfection and melting in my mouth. In no time, foam began to generate from the corners of my lips while glancing over at the small, yet strategically inviting chicken stand.

Once we entered the gates, we were cleared for access and given our assigned area for residence. At that point, three fourths of the Company aviated back to the chicken stand and with eyes that surpassed the capacity of my stomach, I ordered two chicken gyro's and an ice-cold Fanta. Surely it was delicious, but I consumed it so fast that I was unable to taste the seasonings and honestly, I was so excited to enjoy the taste of something supplementary other than the MRE, whatever it tasted like was truly breath taking.

Upon return to the barracks, the Company was separated by Platoons. Headquarters and 1st Platoon occupied the east side of the base

From A Weekend, To A Warzone
Renata Morgan

while 2nd and 3rd Platoons, occupied the north side. The North side was made correlative to town homes with carpet, glass windows and doors that were affixed to each room. On top of all that, they each had their own rest rooms, bedding and of course, the air conditioning just happened to be the greatest amenity of them all.

These accommodations probably wouldn't seem like such a big deal to many, but with temperatures reaching record breaking conditions of 120 degrees or higher during the day, a nice cool atmosphere allowed your soul to regain its life.

My residence was set up on the East and our living quarters were the exact opposite. Although suitable for the occupancy of two, our rooms were deserted and enclosed by four cement walls.

In fact, it was more equivalent to the likes of an impoverished community with generators that ran 24 hour's around the clock and multiple portable potties, positioned outside of the concrete building. On top of that, our nostrils were constantly flamed by the fuming blaze of smoldering hot air, minus the convenience of proper ventilation.

Nevertheless, the current conditions provided more normalcy than what we had previously become accustomed to. Of course, it wasn't the most ideal arrangement, but instead of complaining, my roommate and I, with the help of my Platoon Sergeant spent the majority of our evening carving out wood paneling for 2 window openings and another opening for the door.

Hour's passed, the nightfall bestowed upon us and tirelessly, from all of the exhausting hard work that my energy exerted throughout the day, I embedded myself within the confinement of my personal sleeping area. Unfortunately, I was unable to position myself for comfort and the rest I desired was a long way off. Tossing and turning from the continuance of contracting stomach pains, I began to feel as though I would somehow be delivering a magically conceived baby.

From A Weekend, To A Warzone
Renata Morgan

The pains wouldn't let up and I found myself sporadically running to the restroom, at least three to four times that night. It was a distressed and near disastrous situation, as I barely grasped a hold of the door handle to the portable potty without having an accidental overflow.

Subsequently, daybreak arrived and the consistent reoccurrence of excruciating pain had not let up. At that point, I knew that there was no way I could be on duty to fulfill any missions other than filling out the proper admissions for sick call. Once the paperwork was completed I was taken to the hospital and ironically greeted by half of the Company.

Evidentially, the aroma from the breathtaking chicken stand had us all about to take our last breath because we all ended up diagnosed with a case of food poisoning. I can't speak for anyone else, but besides giving birth that was my first time experiencing something so crucial, pertaining to my stomach.

From A Weekend, To A Warzone
Renata Morgan

After conversing with several other soldiers that had occupied the base prior to our arrival, I was informed about the server's uncleanliness. It turned out that the smell that attracted us Troops was not enough to mask the filthiness of the workers and needless to state, that that was my first and final time consuming any type of food from the economy.

A few days drifted by and I was back to my traditional obligations. My mission consisted of being part of a 3 man search team where we would secure the front gate, checking all vehicles entering and exiting the camp.

The search was very thorough and all individuals would exit the vehicle, to stand approximately 25 feet away while the routine was in progress. One soldier would search the main body inside and outside the vehicle, as well as the hood and undercarriage. The other two soldiers would pull watch over the individuals for security purposes. There would also be an interpreter on standby, in the event that we needed translation conveyed.

From A Weekend, To A Warzone
Renata Morgan

Like clockwork, the searches ran smoothly until one day an Iranian male decided that he wanted to become mildly hostile. On this particular day, I was the one who was conducting the searches. As I proceeded to ask everyone to exit the vehicle and allow me room to search, all but one gentleman obeyed my orders.

I looked at him, he looked back at me and I gestured:
"Move away from the vehicle."

He continued to stand there without the slightest budge and as our eyes locked in pupil to pupil, I felt it was time to call over the interpreter for translation. Interestingly enough, as the interpreter walked up he was unable to get out a syllable before he was cut off by a tone of disgust and disrespect.

"I know exactly what you ordered me to do, but the problem is, I don't take directives from Women."

I looked at him and replied:
"Not only am I a Woman, but I am a Woman with a loaded weapon, who at this time feel

From A Weekend, To A Warzone
Renata Morgan

like my life has been threatened. Now you have a choice, either step back as I asked you to do several times before, or today will be the day you'll get introduced to a real close friend of mine, named nine mille."

As I spoke, I placed my hand on my nine millimeter and he quickly allowed me all the room I needed to complete my search. Needless to state that that was the last time he was seen on the grounds of Camp Caldwell.

My mission of guarding the gate had come to an end, as I was now rotating between the Enemy Prisoner Of War site and alternating inside perimeter assignments. Working the EPW site wasn't that bad because I was on night shift, so instead of 120 degrees, it was a mild 85 degrees nightly. The biggest challenge with this task was the difficulty that I encountered with the stench progressing from the chemical imbalances, airing the inside unit of those that were under surveillance.

From A Weekend, To A Warzone
Renata Morgan

The intensity levels around the camp had leveled out quite a bit and one night while working the sight, my Platoon Sergeant showed up and asked the team if any of us would like to receive a 4 day pass to go home on leave.

"I would **Absolutely** love too."

Of course, that was my first reaction before I recanted with the following statement:

"But I'm telling you right now, if you put me on that plane, the Company will be returning home with one less Soldier than what they left with because there's no way I'm returning once I leave."

I guess my statement must have pondered his brain throughout the night because bright and early the next morning, there was a knock on my door:

"Specialist Morgan, I've come to announce that your leave has been revoked."

From A Weekend, To A Warzone
Renata Morgan

I'm glad he woke up, considering all things with his thinking cap on because I'm certain from the look in my eyes, he realized that the joke would have been on the Company.

Moving forward, the time had come for me to rotate my operation to working the inside perimeter which was a different story, especially being that those were day shift hours. Suited in my desert uniform, my Kevlar and literally the weight of about 30 pounds on my shoulders, (due to the survival tactical vest), I would drive a pace with the fenced area separating the camp and the exterior perimeter.

The 5 O'clock hour was approaching and my team was headed to the fuel point for gas. Suddenly, I began not to feel so well and being the driver, I decided that it would be best for me to alternate my position. I ended up switching out with my gunner who was in the turret, in hopes that I could get some air flow through the sweat pores of my body.

Seconds before pulling up to the fuel point, my body slowly began to slither out the turret and into the back seat of the Humvee.

From A Weekend, To A Warzone
Renata Morgan

"I don't feel good."
Is all I could remember mumbling, before I blacked out into un-consciousness.

When I finally woke up, I looked around and recognized that I was in the hospital. I was dressed in a shirt that was drenched from wetness and a needle from an IV attached to my arm. The more I came to, the more I needed answers and immediately I began calling for the nurse.

"Ms. Morgan, you were brought here because your body was retaining an excessive amount of water which means that your level of salt or sodium had dropped very low, and accidentally over hydrated your system."

"Over hydrated, how was that possible?"

I thought to myself, I didn't know anyone's body could retain enough water to actually have too much water within. It was shocking news, but it was evident and certainly enlightening to me.

From A Weekend, To A Warzone
Renata Morgan

After being released I was instructed to stay inside for the next few days, to allow my body to acclimatize back to its natural state. For me, that was some exciting news because it meant that I would have to be housed on the north side of the base and I was ready to exhaust every bit of the housings accommodating luxury.

Although I absolutely enjoyed every bit of my down time, once I got back in good health I was ready to be released from the confinement of being indoors. My recovery had me locked in for several days and I was ready to feel the sand brushing across my face again.

Due to our mail still being routed to Camp Anaconda, a group of soldiers from the Company would convoy back and forth twice a week to receive incoming packages. I had never been on a mail run since leaving Anaconda, so I figured this would be a good opportunity for me to get out and take part in the pleasures of a day trip.

Normally, we would have the choppers following us via skyline, but activity had settled, so they were on stand down. We were

From A Weekend, To A Warzone
Renata Morgan

traveling with a total of nine soldiers split between three Humvee's to compiled all belongings, and we never made it to the half way point of the journey before encountering an accident.

Out of all days, a tank hit the head of our lead truck and sent the front and rear passenger to seek immediate medical attention. Fortunately, we weren't far from the hospital which allowed us to expedite their urgency to receive care.

As it turned out, the soldiers would be there for some time, so we decided to continue our assignment and recover them on the way back.

Making it safely and free of any engagement for combat, once inside Camp Anaconda we proceeded directly to the Postal Services. The fueling point was the next stop and then the dining facility for lunch, prior to departing for Camp Caldwell.

As we were returning, we stopped back at the sanitarium to retrieve the two soldiers that had been left behind, to receive treatment for the minor bruises sustained. The commute

From A Weekend, To A Warzone
Renata Morgan

was smooth as the wind blew through the windows, creating the stimulation for a light breeze while the radiation began to make its way into the twilight.

Stretching our massive tires across the road ways, we traveled relatively 7 miles from our previous stop and suddenly began to hear sounds that resembled gunshots, from a distance. The next 300 meters they would be heard again, only this time our convoy was the target. Instantly, we had become engaged in warfare with the assassin.

Bullets were flying right above the turret of the Humvee, as we attempted to pursue the direction of gunfire. I was composed as I could possibly be behind the wheel, as salacious words were flying from our mouths in amplitude. It was a visual moment in a world that seemed to be make-believe, as the gunner would be viciously firing off his Mark 19 in automatic burst. In the mean time, I was in steady motion, swerving side to side to avoid direct contact.

"Do You See Anything?"

From A Weekend, To A Warzone
Renata Morgan

Is what I yelled as I proceeded to pull the pant leg of my gunner, but of course with the mixture of commotion the response was unclear.

The shots we not letting up, as we had to radio back to Camp Caldwell for support. However, as the back-up Platoon was en route to provide more weapons and power, they became engaged in battle as well. At this point, you have two Platoons fighting off the enemy and seeking to protect their own lives in the process.

I was doing everything that I could to maintain a sturdy grip in the moment. Speaking as calm as possible with tracer rounds accelerating right in front of my eyes, while I radioed in to the last Platoon to dispatch all soldiers and move out to our locations with intense urgency.

In full blown combat, all three Platoons had left the camp and were facing the opposing side in gun fire, within a 40 miles radius of Camp Caldwell. We had expended all the man power available, but we still had one last resort, THE CHOPPERS.

From A Weekend, To A Warzone
Renata Morgan

After dispensing a massive mound of gun powder and explosives, we finally received the help of our friendly sky accomplice. The Cosmo Warriors came in sure and strong, leaving footprints of missiles as they engaged from the territory of their aerial range.

Upon their arrival, it wasn't long before the extensive sounds had completely stopped as we raced down the main drag, darting into the gates of Camp Caldwell. Shaken up and perplexed, it felt like I had loss my life on 2 to 3 different occasions that day. In fact, I am certain that my heart fell out of my chest countless times, so to make it back into the circumference of what I had known to be my safety grounds, was a joyful relief to my soul.

The Humvee's were damaged and endured several shattered windows from the ricochet of flying bullets, but the fact that we all made it back was a GRATEFUL sensation. Without a doubt we were all engulfed by a whirlwind of emotions, but we were able to take pride in the fact that, EVERY SOLDIER RETURNED UNHARMED.

From A Weekend, To A Warzone
Renata Morgan

That was my first and last time leaving the gates for mail run, until we were disclosing our final farewell. To my surprise, it wasn't long before our opportunity to say Good-Riddance to Camp Caldwell greeted our reality. And just as clear as this moment, I can recall looking back once more at the welcome sign, hoping never to come face to face with such chaos again.

Departing The Middle East

Chapter 8

Energy surfaced the air as the excitement of returning to America approached the journey's end.

November 15th was the last day of our miraculous missions in the homeland of Iraq, and the energy began surfacing through the air from the excitement of returning to America, as the journey's end approached. Indeed, it was time to start completing the exit process, but it wasn't easy.

Once again, over the creeks and through the desert, to the city of Kuwait we traveled as we made our way to Camp Virginia. Upon Arrival, we had to extract all items from the

Renata Morgan

vehicles as they had to be driven to the wash rack before being shipped back to the states.

The wash rack is composed of a huge platform used for washing Military vehicles, as well as other heavy equipment or tools. It is also utilized for removing dirt, chemicals, invasive species and other contaminants with a pressure washer, for the prevention of corrosion that helps to promote longer equipment lifespan.

We spent the entire day, beginning at sun up till sundown, washing every nook and cranny of any dust and dirt out of all vehicle's. If I hadn't been given a lesson 101, on how to thoroughly clean a Humvee, I surely learned that day. There were literally hidden compartments that I had no idea about, packed with globs of dirt and other desert particle's.

Once the Humvee's were cleaned, we were bussed back to the camp where we would be living before our final state of departure. During the waiting period, we were each given a huge foot locker box. The box was approximate to the size of a chest and was to be packed with all of the personal items, that we wanted shipped back to the States. We then had to wait for costumes to come and inspect everything placed in the foot locker, before sending it off.

Prior to the inspection taking place, we were specifically given orders to confirm that there was nothing amongst our possessions, that could cause grounds for confiscation. Against the Commander instructions, one of the inspectors came across a foot locker with some forbidden belongings and made an example out of that soldier.

After seeing what took place, other soldiers in the Company were fighting to place contraband items in the amnesty box. The amnesty box was made available to soldiers for the deposit of prohibited or non-admissible items, prior to inspection or examination.

Once the inappropriate item(s) were placed in the box, the soldiers would no longer be subjected to any terms of discipline. However, that was not the case for the soldier that thought they could out-smart the inspector, by trying to smuggle items taken from Saddam Hussein Palace, but was unsuccessful in doing so.

Although the Palace had been destroyed, there were items that was still in good condition and were stated to be worth riches. Unfortunately, those riches would have that soldier standing in front of a Judge Advocate General, explaining why it was so significant for him to export such items back into the United States.

Stuttering with a loss for words, he just sealed his mouth and dangled his head in shame. Circumstantially, the soldiers plea delayed his mission as he was commanded to stay in the city of Kuwait, for an extra three months.

After appearing in court for a sequence of several hearings, the soldier shamefully received a dishonorable discharge from the Army which ended his Military career. The soldier had four years to go before retirement, and his greed for riches would be the reason that sixteen years of hard work would be seized so abruptly.

November 27th approached, and internally I began to envision myself back home surrounded by family, but in my reality, I was waking up in the whereabouts of tent city. This was the very first time that I had been away from home on Thanksgiving, and it most certainly wouldn't be the same.

The imagination of being in the presence of my Grandmother's home, encircled by my loved ones, with the abundance of love, laughter and some of the best tasting food that this day presented to offer. I was however, fortunate enough to make a phone call and received the overflow of love through the frequency waves.

Despite the circumstances, I was still significantly Blessed beyond measure. My heart was still beating at its normal pace, all five senses that I was born with were still viable to my body. I managed to make it

From A Weekend, To A Warzone
Renata Morgan

through without the detachment of limbs, my ability to think was effectual and most importantly, I was able to express it all.

Yes, I had the opportunity of sitting amongst other soldiers and sharing a nice meal with them. We also enjoyed an opportunity to fellowship, as we reminisced about previous Thanksgiving dinners and how we all wished that we were somewhere other than the desert. And as the day evolved, I was undeterred by everything I had been through because on this day I could not have been more Thankful for anything more, than the sparring of my Life.

It would be several more weeks, that I would spend my days and nights in Camp Virginia. Patiently waiting for our actual exit date, I received the best news as it was announced on December 15th, two weeks prior to Christmas Day. Although, after receiving similar news two times before, it was almost too good to be true.

From A Weekend, To A Warzone
Renata Morgan

The Company was called to a formation and once all the soldiers were accounted for, the news read:

"On this day you have received notification that you'll be departing the country of Iraq within the next 48 hours. When called upon, your Company responded quick and with a purpose. On behalf of the Military Task Force as a whole, We Thank You for all of your hard work and dedication, in supporting us in Operation Iraqi Freedom."

There were so many butterflies soaring on my inside, as I listened to the amazing news being announced. After the dismissal of the formation, I went back to the tent and began packing my belongings right away. My body regained a burst of energy that I hadn't felt in a long time. With a whirlwind of thoughts, I began making plans and thinking about the first thing I was going to engage in, once I landed back in the states.

The Grand Finale

Chapter 9

The buses had arrived at the camp, and the time had finally come for us to be transported to the airport. Once again, we were greeted to customs which took us hours to clear. Then there it was, the waiting process.

We waited several more hours before the wheels of the Boeing 747 eased its way across the airstrip. It wasn't until that point, that I knew that we would Finally be returning to the United States of America.

From A Weekend, To A Warzone
Renata Morgan

Excited and in awe, as this would be my first time flying on such an enormous aircraft. Colossal in stature, equipped with two floors and because we had it all to ourselves, we partied like soldiers just coming back from a deployment.

Due to my lack of rest, by this time my body was functioning in sleep deprivation mode, so when my eyes finally drifted off into dreamland, it was lights out for me. I ended up sleeping for hours on in and by the time I woke up, it was to the sound of the pilot announcing:

"90 minutes before we hit American Soil."

"American Soil",
    I thought to myself, I have been waiting to hear those words for almost a year, and just one week before Christmas Day, they were convincingly broadcasted. Then suddenly, just like that the aircraft was descending, and the pilot slowly lowered the 747 to the ground.

Along with the first sensation of the wheels coming into contact with the ground, the entire plane went wild. There we were, returning to

From A Weekend, To A Warzone
Renata Morgan

the destination where we began the process of preparation that allowed for a successful mission for, "Operation Iraqi Freedom", Ft. Bragg, North Carolina.

When the doors opened, and I reached the last step, I removed myself from the line-up, kneeled down on both knees and kissed the ground, all while giving the Highest Praise.

Despite the fact that we landed back in the United States, we still had one final destination to declare, and that was the distinguished state of Ohio. The Out process through Ft. Bragg was rather expedient which was wonderful because the time was dwindling down with less than a week before Christmas. Of course, we didn't care how long we had to stay up to get thing's completed, we were just excited to get home.

One last time, the wheels would go up as we made preparation to soar through the skies, heading us to the sights of our love ones. Also, another major outlook that I replayed the most, besides seeing my family, was how interesting it was for certain situations to come back full circle because we landed back in my home

From A Weekend, To A Warzone
Renata Morgan

town of Toledo, Ohio seventy-two hours before Christmas. Which just happened to be the exact amount of time we were given before proceeding with our mission, to begin with.

My eyes began glowing as the appearances became flush with the sight of Toledo Metropolitan Airport. The closer we got to landing, my mind went through a shuffle of many different thoughts and the most significant one, was that there was not one family member in sight.

Before leaving Ft. Bragg, I made a call home and had given specific instructions on the place and time of arrival, so I couldn't understand why I wasn't being greeted with the love that I had been waiting nearly a whole year to receive.

Once the official de-boarding process was complete, all the soldiers lined up to stand in their prospective Platoons, as the moment of accountability took place. It was at that point, the Company Commander stood in front of the Company and asked for us to sing the Army song in unison.

From A Weekend, To A Warzone
Renata Morgan

It was an unanticipated request and the initial expectancy of devotion was in-proficient.

"I can't hear you!!!"

The Commander shouted as our tone started out poorly energetic and barely audible.

But as an effort to prevent the entire song from being versed all over again, our vocal vibrations began to increase and as the song came to its end, the energy in the atmosphere shifted. Suddenly there was a door directly in front of us and as it began to slowly rise, our loving families appeared.

There they were, my eyes and heart lit up with extreme excitement and when I tell you that I darted out of that formation faster than a cheetah chasing its prey, it is not a fabrication. Looking swiftly amongst the crowd in search for my family, I caught view of my Mother and as our eyes collided it felt as though my body was moving in slow motion.

It seemed like it took forever for me to reach the side of the room in which they were located, but as I approached, without a word I

From A Weekend, To A Warzone
Renata Morgan

politely extracted my Son from my Mother's arms. In that moment, I held my Son with a maternal endearment while kissing him and weeping with bountiful tears of joy.

My entire family then surrounded me with the love that I had envisioned countless times prior to this moment, as I stood firm to defend this Country.

In conclusion; On behalf of Myself, I would like to Thank the United States Army, for granting me one of the Greatest, most Precious Gifts ever and that was allowing me to be in the presence of My Son and Love ones on December 25th. Truly A Christmas that shall never be forgotten and a Deployment that will Forever be Remembered.

From A Weekend, To A Warzone
Renata Morgan

Acknowledgements

I would first like to give Honor and Thanks to my Heavenly Father, for allowing me to envision such a project that has only been made possible, by His Grace.

I would like to Thank My Mother and Father: for creating such a Beautiful soul and allowing me to develop into an Amazing Woman.

I would like to give Thanks to My Sister: I sincerely appreciate all of the Selfless time shared, through your encouraging words and listening ears. Even in distance, you have been my closest confidant.

To My Brother: Although younger in age, I Thank you for being my protector throughout the years. You have truly inspired me, in ways that you have yet to know.

From A Weekend, To A Warzone
Renata Morgan

To My Brother in Heaven: I shall cherish you and keep you apart of all that I am, as long as my life exists. Your physical presence is absent, but I know that your Angelic Spirit watches over me. Thank You.

To my Entire 323rd Military Police Company: I Thank You All, for the growth, the bonding and for being the baddest Survival of the Fittest Company in our MP Battalion.

To My Editor & Publisher: Thank you for assisting me with the diligent commitment, to bring this vision into its fruition successfully.

To All My Family & Friends: I want to Thank You Sincerely for all of the Love, Support, Encouragement and Prayers throughout my time of Deployment and thereafter.

Last, but Not Least... My Baby: I Love You Son, more than words could ever showcase or describe. I was Blessed to nurture you as a young Prince, and now I am honored to witness your continual development into a Promised King-Manship.

From A Weekend, To A Warzone
Renata Morgan

You have Inspired me in every step of the way and it is because of you that I have and still remain Determined, Powerful, Compassionate, Graceful, Loving and Encouraging with An Abundance of Sanity and Faith.

Also: I would like to Humbly Thank each and every one of You, that has taken a moment to Read My Book, Share My Book or Support My Book In Any Way.

I Appreciate Your Time,
Your Positive Energy, and
Your Seeds Planted,
As Indeed This Is A Vision Secured Within The Soils Of Fertile Grounds,

Sincerely,
Ms. Renata Morgan.